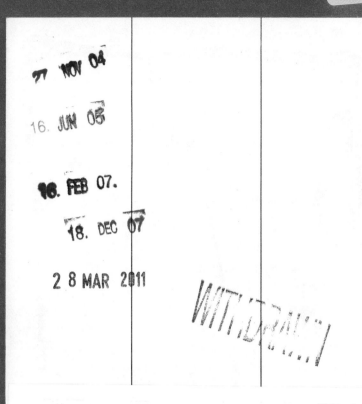

COUNTRYWISE

BRITAIN
PEOPLE • PLACES

Moira Butterfield
and Nicola Wright

Chrysalis Children's Books

Contents

This edition published in 2003 by
Chrysalis Children's Books
64 Brewery Road, London N7 9NT

Copyright © Chrysalis Books PLC

Edited by Nicola Wright and Dee Turner
Designed by Mick McCarthy and Kate Buxton
Cover design by Keren-Orr Greenfeld
Additional illustration by Guy Smith
Typeset by Diane Pullen

A CIP catalogue record for this book is available from the British Library

ISBN 184138 479 8

Printed in China
10 9 8 7 6 5 4 3 2 1

914.2   914.1

About this book

In this book you can find out about the people of Britain and the four countries in which they live – England, Scotland, Wales and Northern Ireland. See how the landscape varies from region to region.

Where Britain is in the world

North America

South America

Europe

Asia

Africa

Australia

Discover too what a typical city and village look like as well as lots of famous places. On page 26 there is a special holiday guide to each country.

Places of interest

Things to see and do

Interesting and fun places to visit are listed, together with details of what they have to offer. There are also some useful addresses for you to contact.

Map of Britain

Britain lies off the coast of mainland Europe. It is made up of four areas: England, Scotland, Wales and Northern Ireland. England, Scotland and Wales are part of an island called Great Britain. Northern Ireland is across the Irish Sea.

 **Longest river:**
The Severn, 354 km. It flows from the Welsh mountains down to south-western England.

Highest mountain:
Ben Nevis, in the Highlands of Scotland, 1,343 m high.

The landscape is very varied, from moors and mountains to meadows and marshes. Some of the world's oldest mountains are in Scotland and Wales.

The Channel Islands (in the English Channel) and the Isle of Man (in the Irish Sea) have their own governments but they are overseen by Britain.

Channel Islands

Sark

Guernsey

Jersey

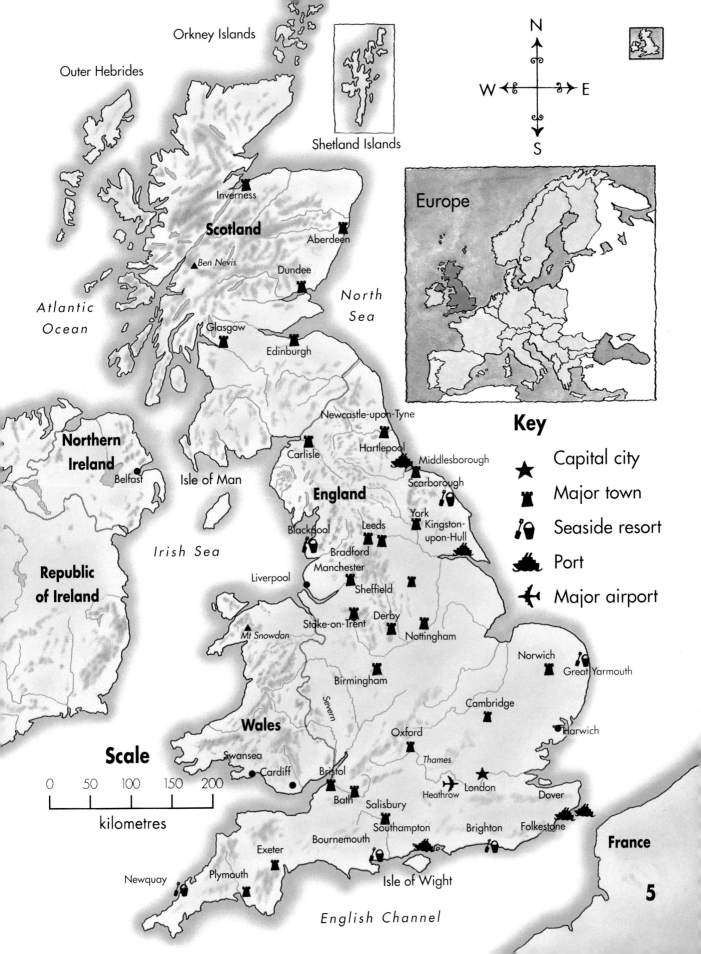

Orkney Islands

Outer Hebrides

Shetland Islands

N
W **E**
S

Europe

Inverness

Scotland

Aberdeen

▲ Ben Nevis

Dundee

North Sea

Glasgow

Edinburgh

Atlantic Ocean

Northern Ireland

Belfast

Isle of Man

England

Newcastle-upon-Tyne

Carlisle

Hartlepool

Middlesborough

Scarborough

York

Kingston-upon-Hull

Key

★ Capital city

♜ Major town

🪣 Seaside resort

⚓ Port

✈ Major airport

Irish Sea

Republic of Ireland

Blackpool

Leeds

Bradford

Liverpool

Manchester

Sheffield

Stoke-on-Trent

Derby

Nottingham

▲ Mt Snowdon

Birmingham

Norwich

Great Yarmouth

Cambridge

Severn

Wales

Oxford

Harwich

Thames

Scale

0   50   100   150   200

kilometres

Swansea

Cardiff

Bristol

Bath

Salisbury

Southampton

London

Heathrow

Dover

Brighton

Folkestone

France

Bournemouth

Exeter

Newquay

Plymouth

Isle of Wight

English Channel

5

Facts about Britain

Britain and Northern Ireland are quite crowded compared with other European countries. On average, there are 230 people living in every square kilometre. England is the most crowded part of the British Isles.

 Size: 242,534 sq km

 Population: 55,487,000

 Capital city: London

The British flag is called the 'Union flag'. It combines the crosses of St George (England, St Andrew (Scotland), and St Patrick (Ireland). It is also sometimes known as the 'Union Jack'.

Union flag

England

Scotland

Ireland

Official name: United Kingdom of Great Britain and Northern Ireland.

The Head of State is the Queen or King. She or he inherits the title, and so is not elected by the people. The government is made up of Members of Parliament, who are elected.

Language

The official language is English, but there are some other languages spoken, too.

The Gaelic language is still used in parts of the Scottish Highlands and islands.

The Welsh language is spoken in some parts of Wales.

People who move to Britain are often bilingual. Indian and Pakistani children learn their own languages as well as English.

Money

British money is divided into pounds (£) and pence (p).
100 pence equal 1 pound.

Here are some of the famous people who appear on British banknotes:

£20 Edward Elgar
(famous composer)

£10 Charles Darwin
(famous writer)

£5 Elizabeth Fry
(prison reformer)

Coins are made in amounts of 1, 2, 5, 10, 20 and 50 pence and 1 pound.

Some things Britain is well-known for

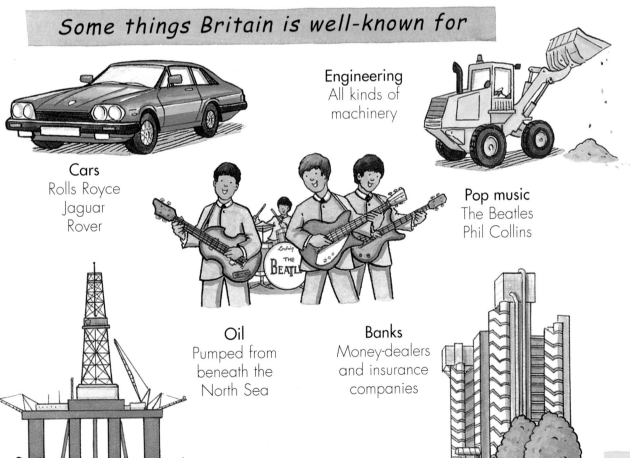

Engineering
All kinds of machinery

Cars
Rolls Royce
Jaguar
Rover

Pop music
The Beatles
Phil Collins

Oil
Pumped from beneath the North Sea

Banks
Money-dealers and insurance companies

Regions of Britain

Although Britain is small, its scenery varies from region to region. Most of the high mountains are in the north and west. It is flattest in the south and east.

Much of Scotland is rugged, empty moorland. Over half of Britain's forests are found here.

The mountains of Scotland provide a home for animals such as wild cats, deer and birds of prey.

In eastern England the land is flat and sometimes marshy.

The south-west of England has the mildest weather. Here there are plenty of sandy holiday beaches.

The British climate is never very hot or very cold. Generally, but not always, it is warmest in the south. The weather changes from day to day. Rain falls all year round.

Wales is a country of hills and mountains. The highest mountain is Snowdon, in the north-west.

Farming is important all over Britain.

There are thousands of small farms in Northern Ireland. Most farmers grow crops and keep animals.

Sheep and beef cattle are kept in the north and in Wales.

Crops are mostly grown in the east and south.

Fruit is grown in southern parts of England.

Dairy cows are most common in the south-west.

9

London

London is Britain's capital, and its biggest city. It is the centre of government and business.

The Romans founded London in AD 43. They set up camp and built a bridge over the River Thames. The city gradually grew up along the banks of the river.

You can get around the city in a black London taxi ...

... or by tube train (the first underground railway system in the world) ...

... or on a red double-decker bus.

London has many parks. Some of the parks are royal – which means that they belong to the monarch, although all people can visit them. Hyde Park is the largest and has a lake.

Famous buildings

Natural History Museum
(one of London's biggest museums. It has lots of working exhibits for children.)

(begun almost 1,000 years ago, this is where all English kings and queens are crowned.)

Covent Garden
(surrounded by theatres, restaurants and shops. Street entertainers perform for passers-by.)

(home of the Royal Family.)

St Paul's Cathedral
(designed by Christopher Wren, it has the heaviest bell in Britain.)

Tower of London
(once a prison for traitors. The British Crown Jewels are kept here.)

Houses of Parliament
(home of the British government. It has the famous Big Ben clock.)

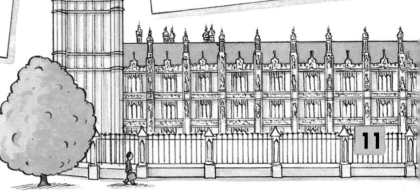

In a typical city

Modern shopping precinct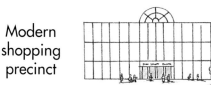

Double-decker bus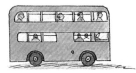

Fountain

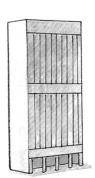

Office block

Cafés and bars

Historic archway for a coach and horses

Most British cities have grown up gradually over the centuries. You can often see a mixture of old and new buildings.

Cathedral

Advertisement hoarding

HEAT→ ELECTRIC

Town hall

Park

Statue of famous person

Restaurant

Radio/television tower

Theatre

Cinema complex

Old, narrow, cobbled street

In a typical village

There are many different kinds of village in Britain. Each has its own history, often going back hundreds of years. Here are some things to look out for.

Often there is a big manor house, where the local wealthy landowner lived.

Old school

Market cross, where a market took place

Old water trough and pump

Some villages are built around a patch of grass called a green. Sometimes there is a pond, once the main water supply.

Look at plaques and memorials inside churches for clues about the history of a village.

Cottages are usually made from local stone. Here are some different cottages:

Crofts, found in Scotland and Ireland.

Box-framed cottage made from plaster in a wooden frame.

Thatched cottage with a roof made from reeds or straw.

Almshouses, built for the poor.

Pub sign

Village sign

What people do

Britain is a very crowded island. Most people live in towns and cities, where there are many factories and offices.

Factories, mills, mines and engineering works provide people with jobs.

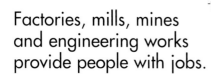

The older industries of iron, coal and steel, ship building and textiles do not employ as many people as they used to.

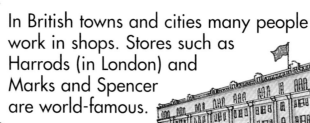

In British towns and cities many people work in shops. Stores such as Harrods (in London) and Marks and Spencer are world-famous.

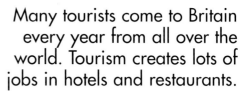

Over two thirds of the British workforce are in 'service' industries, such as law, banking and insurance.

Many tourists come to Britain every year from all over the world. Tourism creates lots of jobs in hotels and restaurants.

The leisure industry is growing in Britain.

Britain's roads, railways and airports provide jobs.

Heathrow Airport, near London, is one of the world's busiest airports, handling about 38 million people a year.

The Channel Tunnel, underneath the English Channel, links Britain to the rest of Europe.

Many people work for the government. Policemen, teachers, doctors and nurses are examples.

People in Britain produce electronics, plastics, medicines, pottery, glass and books.

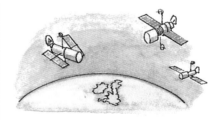

Britain also makes many aircraft and space satellites.

Festivals

Festivals and celebrations are held all over Britain throughout the year. Here are some of the most famous.

On 5 November people celebrate Guy Fawkes's Night with fireworks and bonfires. Guy Fawkes tried to blow up the Houses of Parliament in 1605, but he was caught just as he was about to set light to the gunpowder. Children often make a 'Guy' out of old clothes and burn him on top of a bonfire.

In August the Edinburgh Festival takes place. There are lots of plays, concerts, exhibitions and a military display in the castle called the 'tattoo'.

Scottish people celebrate Burns Night on 25 January, the anniversary of the birth of Scottish poet Robert Burns in 1759.

The Eisteddfod music and poetry festival is held in Wales in August.

Northern Ireland's oldest country fair, Oul Lammas, is held in Ballycastle each summer. There are lots of farm animals on show and hundreds of stalls selling goods.

Hallowe'en is celebrated on the night of 31 October. People dress up in scary costumes, as witches and ghosts. They play traditional games including apple bobbing (picking up apples in the mouth from a bowl of water).

April Fools' Day, the first day of April, is when people in Britain play practical jokes on each other.

May Day is a traditional springtime celebration. Often a May queen is chosen and there are dances around a Maypole.

Major sporting events

Oxford and Cambridge boat race – March

Wimbledon tennis championship – June

Cricket test matches – throughout the summer

Grand National horse race – April

Scottish highland games – throughout the summer

F.A. Cup football matches – throughout the winter

History of Britain

AD 43

A Roman villa

The Romans arrived in England, where they ruled for nearly 400 years. They also conquered parts of Wales, but not Scotland or Ireland. They built towns, roads, villas and forts.

◄

1066

William the Conqueror invaded from France and became King William I of England. The years from this time until 1485 are called the Middle Ages. Abbeys and monasteries were very important during this period. ►

1485-1603

Elizabeth I (queen 1558– 1603)

Henry VIII (king 1509– 1547)

◄

From 1485 to 1603 the Tudor family ruled England. Henry VIII (1491–1657) broke away from the Roman Catholic Church and destroyed many monasteries. During his daughter's reign (Elizabeth I, 1558–1603) Shakespeare wrote his plays.

1603-1714

Charles I

In 1603 James Stuart became King of Scotland and England. He united the two countries. His son Charles I was beheaded during the English Civil War. His grandson Charles II restored the monarchy to Britain in 1660.

►

1714-1837

George I ▲

George I came to the throne in 1714. He was succeeded by George II, III and IV, and then William IV. During this time Britain became rich and powerful.

Queen Victoria ruled for over 60 years. During her long reign, Britain changed a great deal. Many factories and railways were built. Many cities grew much bigger because people moved in from the countryside to find work.

▼

1837-1901

1914-18

During World War I Britain, France, Russia and their allies fought Germany and Austria. Many soldiers were killed before Germany was defeated. ▲

1939-45

During World War II Britain and its allies fought Germany and Japan. Some British cities were heavily bombed and had to be rebuilt after the war. Food was rationed. ▶

1973

Britain joined the European Community (EC), a group of European countries who work together to make laws, trade agreements and economic policies. ◀

Famous places

There are many interesting and historic places to visit all around Britain. Here are a few of the most famous tourist attractions.

There are lots of castles in Britain. Windsor Castle overlooks the River Thames and is one of the biggest. Kings and queens have lived there for 900 years.

There was a big fire at Windsor Castle in 1992.

Stonehenge is a mysterious circle of huge stones put there over 4,000 years ago.

Britain has many fine old churches and cathedrals. Salisbury Cathedral has the highest spire.

The City of Bath was founded by the Romans. You can visit the Roman baths. Hot water bubbles up into them from an underground stream.

In Wales you can walk on the hills or climb the mountains of Snowdonia. There is much unspoiled countryside and beautiful scenery.

England is famous for its stately homes. Many of them are open to the public. Longleat in Wiltshire is one of the most popular tourist attractions in the country.

There is a safari park in the beautiful grounds of Longleat.

Cornwall is famous for warm, sunny weather, sandy beaches and coastal walks. It also has a famous ruined castle, Tintagel, said by some to be the home of King Arthur.

Some more famous places

York, in northern England, was a very important Roman city. Later, about 1,000 years ago, it was taken over by Viking invaders from Scandinavia. You can see how the Vikings lived when you visit the special museum called the Jorvik Centre. The sights, sounds and even the smells of Viking life have been recreated.

The Giant's Causeway is on the coast of Northern Ireland. It is made up of thousands of rock columns made of hardened lava like stepping stones.

Stratford-on-Avon, in central England, was the birthplace of the playwright William Shakespeare. His wife Anne Hathaway's cottage is open to the public.

You can take a boat trip on Loch Ness in Scotland. It is world-famous for its legendary monster, which some people claim to have seen.

The Cheddar Gorge in south-west England stretches for about 2.5 km and has cliffs over 120 m high. There are lots of rare plants and animals to see.

Lake Windermere is the biggest lake in England. You can take boat trips on it or walk on the hills around, in the beautiful Lake District.

Lindisfarne is an island off the north-east coast of England. You can walk across to it at low tide to see the old priory, castle and nature reserve. At other times it is completely surrounded by sea.

At Ironbridge Gorge, in central England, you can see the first iron bridge in the world, built in 1779. Around it there are museums that explain how industry has grown during the last 200 years. There are also mills and mines to visit.

England

On the following pages there are lots of suggestions for visits around Britain.

Check opening days and times before you visit.

Outer London

Epping Forest
Lots of ponds, lakes and woodland wildlife. Visit the Forest Museum.

Greenwhich
Home of the National Maritime Museum. Visit the *Cutty Sark* tea-clipper, which stands on a quay on the River Thames nearby.

Richmond Park
A large park with herds of deer.

Hampton Court Palace
A Tudor palace with a famous maze in the grounds and (it is said) ghosts in the house. ▼

Syon Park
A motor museum, a conservatory full of jungle plants and a collection of living butterflies.

Kew Gardens
Huge botanical gardens with thousands of rare plants and trees, hothouses and a pagoda. ▼

Thames Barrier
The world's biggest movable flood gate. Take a boat trip around it.

South-west England

Bath, Avon
See page 22.

Beaulieu, Hampshire
See hundreds of vintage vehicles at the motor museum.

Bristol, Avon
Home of the SS *Great Britain*, the world's first iron ship. You can also visit Bristol Zoo.

Cheddar Gorge
See page 25.

Dartmoor and Exmoor National Parks, Devon
Acres of heathland, ideal for hiking or pony-trekking.

Land's End, Cornwall
The most westerly point of mainland Britain. Steep cliffs overlook the Atlantic Ocean.

Longleat, Wiltshire
See page 23.

Salisbury, Wiltshire
See page 22.

Stonehenge, Wiltshire
See page 22.

St Michael's Mount, Cornwall
At low tide you can walk out to the island to see the castle. ▼

Tintagel, Cornwall
See page 23.

Wookey Hole Caves, Somerset
Deep caves once inhabited by Stone Age people.

Yeovilton Fleet Air Arm Museum, Somerset
Collection of naval aircraft, together with the original Concorde.

South-east England

Battle, Sussex
Site of the Battle of Hastings in 1066. See the ruins of William the Conqueror's abbey.

Blenheim Palace, Oxfordshire
Home of the Dukes of Marlborough. The beautiful gardens are famous.

Brighton, Sussex
Seaside resort with a marina, sealife centre, beaches and a pier. Also Brighton Pavilion, once a royal palace. ▼

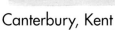

Canterbury, Kent
Famous cathedral, scene of Thomas à Becket's murder in 1170.

Isle of Wight
Nature trails, beaches, a Roman villa and Osborne House, Queen Victoria's holiday home.

▲

New Forest, Hampshire
Once a royal hunting forest, now inhabited by the famous New Forest ponies.

Oxford, Oxfordshire
Famous for its ancient University colleges, libraries and museums. You can also go punting on the river.

Portsmouth, Hampshire
Visit HMS Victory, Nelson's flagship at the Battle of Trafalgar (1805), and other historic ships.

Windsor, Berkshire
See page 22.

Woburn Abbey, Bedfordshire
Eighteenth-century abbey and wildlife park.

Central England

Alton Towers, Staffordshire
Britain's biggest theme park. Lots of fairground rides and fun activities.

▼

Chedworth, Gloucestershire
Roman villa with mosaics.

Cotswolds
Area of natural beauty. Visit the Cotswold Farm Park with its collection of rare breeds of farm animals.

Forest of Dean, Gloucestershire
A mysterious forest criss-crossed by paths, with castles and an abbey.

Ironbridge, Yorkshire
See page 25.

▲

Lincoln, Lincolnshire
Lincoln Cathedral and Roman remains to see.

Malvern Hills, Worcestershire
A range of hills that are good for walking along. There is also an Iron Age fort to visit.

Stratford-on-Avon, Warwickshire
See page 24.

England

Eastern England

Cambridge, Cambridgeshire
An ancient University city. You can go boating on the River Cam.

Ely, Cambridgeshire
Famous cathedral associated with Saxon nobleman Hereward the Wake.

Grimes Graves, Norfolk
Prehistoric flint mines to explore.

Norfolk Broads
A network of waterways ideal for boating.

Norfolk coast
Creeks and marshes, beaches and estuaries. Good for birdwatching.

Norwich, Norfolk
Cathedral town with narrow, medieval streets.

Otter Trust, Bungay, Suffolk
Otters are reared here to preserve the species.

Peterborough, Cambridgeshire
Cathedral city where Mary Queen of Scots is buried.

Northern England

Blackpool, Lancashire
A seaside resort famous for its funfair attractions, high tower and nighttime 'illuminations'.

Conisbrough, Yorkshire
A big castle with a Norman tower.

Flamborough Head, Humberside
A lighthouse, seabird colonies, nature trails and cliff-top walks.

Hadrian's Wall, Northumberland
Remains of a long Roman frontier wall. You can visit fort remains and museums along the 117 km route.

Isle of Man
Beaches, nature trails, mountain railway and the world's biggest water wheel.

Lake District, Cumbria
See page 25.

Levens Hall, Cumbria
Elizabethan house with gardens and a museum of working steam engines.

Lindisfarne, Northumberland
See page 25.

Northumberland coast
Boat trips to see the seals and bird colonies. Fishing villages and cliff-top castles.

Northumberland National Park
Fell-walking country.

Scarborough, Yorkshire
A popular seaside resort with lots to see and do.

York, Yorkshire
See page 24.

Scotland

Antonine Wall
The remains of the wall that once marked the northern edge of the Roman Empire. Visit the best-preserved part at Rough Castle near Bonnybridge.

Aviemore, Highland
Scotland's main winter sports resort near the Cairngorm mountains.

Balmoral, Grampian
You can look round the castle when the Royal Family are not in residence.

Beinn Eighe Nature Trail, Highland
Home of the Golden Eagle.

Ben Nevis, Highland
The highest mountain in Britain.

Burns's cottage, Strathclyde
Childhood home of the famous Scottish poet Robert Burns.

Cairnholy, Dumfries and Galloway
Prehistoric burial mounds with nearby runs at Threave Castle and Sweetheart Abbey.

Caledonian canal, Highland
You can hire boats to travel along this 96 km waterway.

Craigievar Castle, Grampian
A huge castle with lots of towers and turrets, winding stairs and a great hall.

Culloden, Highland
Site of the Battle of Culloden in 1746, the last battle on British soil. There is a visitor centre and battlefield trail.

Culsh, Grampian
Take a torch to explore the dark passageways of this prehistoric 'earthhouse'.

Loch Ness
See page 24.

Drumlanrig Castle, Dumfries and Galloway
Dramatic castle with nature trails and an adventure playground.

Edinburgh
See page 18.

Forth Road Bridge, Central
A large suspension bridge spanning the Firth of Forth.

Glamis Castle, Tayside
A castle reputedly haunted by nine ghosts, including Macbeth.

Glasgow, Strathclyde
A lively city with a medieval cathedral and lots of exhibitions and museums.

Inverness, Highland
One of Scotland's oldest towns. Nearby Cawdor Castle has a drawbridge and nature trails.

Isle of Skye, Hebrides
Most famous of the islands. Spectacular scenery, castles and woollen mills to visit.

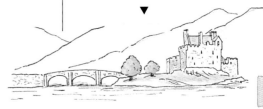

Wales

Borth, Dyfed
Sand dunes and a nature trail. At low tide a submerged forest can be seen.

Brecon Beacons, Powys
As well as walks there are caves and a dinosaur park. ▼

Caerleon, Gwent
Remains of a Roman legionary fortress.

Caernarfon Castle, Gwynedd
Impressive castle where Prince Charles was made Prince of Wales. ▼

Cardiff
The busy capital city of Wales. There is lots to see including a ruined castle and the Museum of Wales. ▼

Dolaucothi, Dyfed
Roman gold mines to explore.

▲

Gower Peninsula, West Glamorgan
An area of natural beauty. Caves to explore and birds to spot.

Harlech Castle, Gwynedd
Ruined castle stronghold on cliffs overlooking a beautiful beach and sand dunes.
▼

Llandrindod Wells, Powys
Visit the Doll Museum.

Llandudno, Gwynedd
Seaside resort. Britain's longest cablecar ride to the top of the cliff, called the Great Orme.

Menai Bridge, Gwynedd
Museum of Childhood with lots of toys and games.

Pembrokeshire National Park, Dyfed
Cliffs, bays, headlands and beaches. There is an information centre at Broad Haven.

St David's, Dyfed
The smallest cathedral city in Britain. Nearby Whitesands Bay is a good beach for surfing.

Saint Fagan's, South Glamorgan
Welsh Folk Museum, including a farmhouse, cottage, tollhouse, woollen and corn mills.

Severn Bridge, linking England and Wales
It is the second largest bridge in Britain. Visit the ruins of nearby Chepstow Castle. ▼

Snowdonia, Gwynedd
See page 23. You can reach the top of Mount Snowdon by mountain railway.

Tintern Abbey, Gwent
You can walk round the impressive ruins of the monastery which was destroyed by Henry VIII.

Northern Ireland

Armagh
Visit the city's two beautiful cathedrals and the planetarium.

Bangor, County Down
A popular seaside resort with a small harbour.

Belfast, Antrim
Ulster Folk and Transport Museum and the large city hall styled on St Paul's Cathedral.

Carnfunnock Country Park, Antrim
The park's maze is shaped like the map of Ireland. There's also a playground, crafts exhibition and picnic site.

Carrickfergus Castle, Antrim
The castle faces Belfast Lough. It has played a large part in Irish history.

Castle Ward, County Down
An eighteenth-century mansion on the shores of a lake. There is a ruined abbey nearby.

Giant's Causeway, Antrim
See page 24.

Glens, Antrim
A group of beautiful glens. See the fantastic waterfall at Glenariff glen.

Lough Erne, Fermanagh
You can take a ferry trip out on the lough to Devenish Island to see the old stone carvings.

Marble Arch Caves, Fermanagh
Lots of underground caves with large stalagmites and stalagtites.

Roe Valley Country Park, Fermanagh
The park is full of wild plants and animals. There is a visitors' centre where you can learn all about the park's history and legends.

Shane's Castle Railway, Antrim
Ride on the steam railway through woods and along the banks of Lough Neagh (the largest lake in Britain) to Shane's Castle.

Strangford Lough, County Down
This seawater lough is joined to the Irish Sea. You can see many rare seabirds and marine animals.

Tollymore Forest Park, County Down
The park is set in the beautiful Mourne Mountains. You can go pony-trekking, fishing and walking.

Ulster American Folk Museum, Tyrone
Learn about the links with America through Irish settlers there.

Useful addresses

English Tourist Board
Thames Tower
Black's Road
Hammersmith
LONDON W6 9EL

(0207) 730 3488

Scottish Tourist Board
23 Ravelston Terrace
EDINBURGH
EH4 3EU

(0131) 332 2433

The Wales Tourist Board
Brunel House
2 Fitzalan Road
CARDIFF
CF2 1UY

(01222) 499909

Northern Ireland Tourist Board
59 North Street
BELFAST
BT1 1ND

(01232) 231221